ELEVEN
TWO
SEVEN

My Story of God's Grace

Daniel Scott Blüst

ISBN 978-1-0980-5158-7 (paperback)
ISBN 978-1-0980-5159-4 (digital)

Christian Faith Publishing, Inc.
832 Park Avenue
Meadville, PA 16335
www.christianfaithpublishing.com

Printed in the United States of America

To my parents, who put up with many sleepless nights, I am thankful that they got to see my life turn around. My children, who had to face a dad who was not what they deserved. My wife, Shana, who has stood beside me through this surreal transformation. And to everyone who prayed for me while I was doing life on my own terms.

I have many memories of the early years of my life. As I have reflected and pondered on them, it is obvious that I was being set up for the life I am living today. Being molded and shaped by every experience, every wound had its place, and every bad decision would be a testimony to the redeeming power of God's grace. One of the earliest memories I have was of my fourth or fifth birthday party. It was my first realistic encounter with the spiritual world. I was inside of the house, spying on everyone from the window of my parent's bedroom when out of the closet, there appeared what would be an older woman. She tried to convince me to take her hand and come with her by saying that my mom said it was okay. I remember the fear that filled my heart as I ran out of the room to find my parents. I found my dad and told him what happened. He went into the house to look for the old woman and not surprisingly found nothing.

I had nightmares and visions as a child where the characters on my bedsheets would come to life and speak to me. It was written off as my imagination back then, but as I look back from my calling, it was clearly the beginning of my spiritual battle. It wasn't all scary though; my childhood was better than most. I lived a pretty normal life for a kid growing up in the seventies. We seldom went to church though, the typical creasters, you know, Christmas and Easter. I often say that was more of a blessing than anything. I never learned any religion or churchy stuff. We did have one of those S&H Green Stamp pictures of Jesus hanging in our living room though. I never doubted that there was a God. I just grew up to hate Him.

Rebellion was a part of my character from early on. My parents would tell a story of when I was three, where my grandfather took my favorite teddy bear from me and put it in his shirt pocket. My response to him was, "I'm gonna kick your ass!" Yep, I was three with a twelve-year-old brother and sister (twins) and an eleven-year-old sister. I learned the finer part of the English language before I even got to school and became fluent by the second grade. I remember standing at the end of the driveway, giving the neighbors the middle finger while shouting out the explanation of what that was supposed to mean.

Later on in life, I would get that saying tattooed inside my lower lip. I also developed a love for beer and the fearless frequency of playing with matches. From stealing people's beer at birthday parties to burning the hair off of my sister's Barbie dolls, to flashing the neighbor girls, there wasn't a dull moment in elementary school. From sixth grade to eighth grade, I was overweight. I graduated from huskies to men's pants by thirteen, which lead to a lot of bullying and rejection from schoolmates.

I can vividly remember laying in my front yard, crying, thinking that I would never have a girlfriend. I told my parents that I was going to live with them forever. That didn't take long to change, but I always seemed to end up back at their house throughout the years.

My eighth grade summer, I began to slim down and landed my first girlfriend. She motivated me to get into shape but dumped me before school even started. As they say, the first cut is the deepest. I had no problem getting girlfriends after that, but between my anger and insecurities, I always found a way to mess it up. I also managed to take that into my adult life. As messed up as I was, I always managed to get good grades with little effort. What a gift that God gave me, the ability to see something and remember it. Most everything that I ever did was either self-taught or with minimal training, not a good combination for a National Honor Society student with evil influence. Apart from sex, drugs, cars, and rock and roll, high school was pretty uneventful. A few tussles and a couple of girlfriends and I was out of school and ready to take on the world. Believe me, I gave it a good run.

Right out of high school, I started my own business. Normal jobs didn't go too well for me up until then. Fired for stealing or going to work high kept me from digging into a career. My first job as a contractor was building an addition for a guy in my old neighborhood. Not dedicated enough and the guy short-paying me was enough to go back to the grind. I did some tree work with my best friend for a while. We worked for a small tree company where we were high most of the time. An injury to my eye cut that short, so I started working for a discount grocery store. That was where I really started raising hell. Getting drunk, doing drugs, sleeping with customers and cashiers, and staying out all night, I dumped most of my money into my car making it go as fast as it could.

One night, while hanging out at the local gathering place where we would set up our street races, I met the sister of one of the guys who would street race with us. Her dad was a street racer too, so she was into the same scene as I was into. We started dating the summer before her senior year of high school, and by the next spring, I got her pregnant. We decided to get married a couple weeks before her graduation to get ready for our little family. The odds were stacked against us, but that was right up my alley. We were young, broken, and didn't have a clue what the world was about. We brought a daughter into the mess early that December. We fought a lot, but we somehow stuck it out. Drinking beer, watching races, working full time, and barely making ends meet. It wasn't too long before I was messing around. Nothing serious, just some flirting and dirty talk, just enough to kill the pain of a struggling marriage. We climbed our way up the ladder at work and began to make more money, but just like everyone else, we just ended up spending more. I spent a lot of time with her family hunting, fishing, and doing the car thing. Her dad wasn't the best example of a husband. He had his side fling going on. That kind of helped me feel a little better with my situation. We lived that way for years, and as the money would increase, we would move up the ranks of the Jones'.

Our daughter was growing up fast, and everything was going smooth until I got sick in 1995. I wasn't feeling good for a few days, having trouble eating and such. After a few tests, it was determined that I had Crohn's disease.

An autoimmune disease that attacks the digestive system causing inflammation, blockages, and even holes throughout the digestive system. The side effects can be just as bad, from severe arthritis, loss of vision, skin diseases, and without absorbing the proper nutrients, organs can shut down, inevitably ending in death. It was a blow to me and our family. I was in pain for months and had to have my gallbladder removed. I was pissed off at God and vowed that if I ever got better, I was going to live each day like it was my last. Better I got, and that I did.

It was nearly a year later after GI bleeds, medicine that made my hair fall out, many pain-filled days, and one near suicide attempt that I was feeling back to normal. The near suicide attempt came after I put my daughter on the bus and having terrible pain. I sat on my bedside with my .357 in my hand, thinking how much better I would feel without the pain. I put the barrel in my mouth and looked up to see a picture of my daughter staring back at me. I broke down into tears, thinking how I would miss watching her grow up and how she would be devastated to come home to her dead father. I put the gun away and laid there in pain as the tears gradually came to an end. But I was finally out of the woods and ready to live it up. I got promoted at work and assigned to a new store. More money and more authority.

I was feeling good and making good money and off to the races. I bought a Harley, a guitar, started a band, and picked up a couple of girlfriends. We even bought our dream house, a nice place with some woods, and everything we thought we wanted. Another Harley and a Z-28, and it still wasn't enough. The band was rolling. We recorded our first CD and playing in clubs around the Harrisburg area. More drugs, more alcohol, more women.

With everything going on, I can honestly say our marriage didn't get any worse. The stuff we had kept us occupied, but we were far from happy. My life was a mess, and it was starting to show. I ended up in anger management after a customer complaint turned into me telling her to f——— off, and I threw a case of paper at a member of upper management. I got emotionally attached to an employee whom I slept with, and that was pressing me even harder. With all of that going on, it was decided to transfer me to another store, one at the bottom of the barrel.

Always up for a challenge, I went in with guns blazing. I met a new drug supplier, found a few new girlfriends, and began to take the store from the bottom of the barrel to the top in the district. The band was playing weekly, and things were smoothing out at home. Until one day at work, an old friend of mine came in looking for something for their office with the owner of the Harley shop he worked for. Within a week, I was offered a job at the shop, selling motorcycles. That's all I needed to hear after ten years of retail management, I was out of there. The Harley shop fed all of my inner demons. There were plenty of tough guys to push my anger to a new level. There were enough drug users and dealers to get me higher than ever before. The money was better, and the women were easier. I was living the dream, and there wasn't a movie that could be made to portray the craziness I was living. The band was getting better gigs in the motorcycle community, and we were moving up to better things. I learned my lesson getting emotionally involved with other women. I decided that quantity was better than quality.

One night, before a big gig for the band, a buddy and I took the Harley's out for a few drinks and a little action. We got smashed and picked up a couple of women at one of the bars. We went back to the one woman's apartment and didn't end up leaving until the next morning. I rolled into work and the gig smelling like a rough night. Neither my bandmates nor my wife found my MIA status very amusing. I slept with a few customers and coworkers over the next month and was starting to show up to work higher and higher. I was making all kinds of enemies everywhere I went, from my daughter's dentist, my boss, certain tough guys, my band, and, of course, my wife. Everyone was a jerk but me. I couldn't believe it.

A new girl started at the shop over in the offices. She was friendly and drawn to the lifestyle. We started talking and decided we would set up a date behind our spouses' backs. The date went as we thought it would, except she ended up getting pregnant. I can remember the feeling I had when she told me. It was that feeling you get when you fly past a cop at ninety miles per hour. You don't know that feeling? It is one hundred times more intense than "uh-oh." We discussed how we would handle it, and she was willing to play it off as her and her husband's. As crappy of a human being as I was, I couldn't fathom having a child out there not knowing I was their father. I was sick to my stomach and could barely face my wife and daughter. I hid it for a little while, but after a family night out, watching *Lilo and Stitch*, my breakdown came to a head.

I ended up telling my wife and daughter. As expected, they were devastated. My wife said she was willing to work through it, but I knew that was just asking for all kinds of dysfunction. I walked out the door that day, September 13, 2002. I was crushed with guilt and shame. My heart was shattered into pieces, but nothing like the hearts of my daughter and my wife. The other woman left her husband, and we moved in together. It was intense, more drugs, more anger, more stress, and not much of hope for my future.

The band broke up, and my job was getting harder and harder. My wife and I would fight over the phone, my daughter and I would cry over the phone, and home was just as bad. My girlfriend was being taken to court over custody of her daughter, fighting with her husband, and getting bigger by the day. We fought every day. I would literally beat on myself until I was bleeding and black and blue. We couldn't pay our bills and had trouble keeping food on the table because drug use and legal costs were taking a toll on us. And then our son was born. He was a sickly baby spending his first days in the NICU. It made a hard situation that much harder. I was so messed up at work that they implemented a drug policy which sent me to rehab. I ended up leaving the rehab which was the condition for keeping my job.

After failing a second drug test, I quit just minutes before being fired, which was bound to happen between the repossession company stalking me to get my motorcycle and an escalating battle with some tough guys. I was more of a liability than an asset. Unemployed and messed up in the head, I was a ticking time bomb.

One day, I was out front of our place and ran into one of my neighbors. We got talking, and it turned out that he was fresh out of prison and working for a local independent cycle shop. A couple days later, I started working there with him. This was when life became real. (What I mean was the drugs were harder, the tough guys got tougher, and the guns were no longer for hunting.) We were high on cocaine and making a mess of everything we came in contact with. My girlfriend and I would be up for days on cocaine, and our fights became physical.

My new partner in crime and I decided it would be better to open our own shop than make this other guy all of the money. We packed up shop and moved into our own place. We did what we had to make it work. We were collecting debts the hard way, dealing cocaine to support our habits, and making the motorcycle business famous with the community (which hated us) and the police (which followed us everywhere). Neither one slowed us down a bit.

I left my girlfriend and son behind and became a full-time nomad. When we would sleep, it would be at the shop or a stranger's couch. We partied constantly with other dealers, prostitutes, and any junky who thought they could hang with us. That lifestyle was taking a toll on me. We were being taken to court for operating our business in improper zoning, and the line between ally and enemy was getting blurred. Undercover police would frequent our shop and young girls with daddy issues were doing anything and everything to be a part of our circus. We had a close friend leave our shop and get killed in a motorcycle accident and a few others head off to prison. One night, while we were partying with some young girls, the police showed up. It turned out that they were just there to take advantage of the one girl who was messed up on cocaine and whiskey. No joke, the cop took her off, had sex, and dropped her back off. After that, I had enough. The demons I saw during that time were the darkest I had ever seen up to that point. I decided that I would go get a personal part of my body tattooed to keep the women away, and just maybe I would get some sleep.

After meeting with my tattoo artist, he decided that my new design didn't fit within the boundary of our relationship. As the devil would have it, when I got back to our cycle shop, there was a girl hanging out with my partner. I told him what happened at the tat shop and wouldn't you know it, her roommate was a tattoo artist, a female who was willing to do the tattoo. Two days later, we headed to their apartment to get the tattoo done and party. She was young and attractive, but I seriously was on a sabbatical from dating.

A couple days later, she called the shop and asked if we could all hang out again. We were heading to court the next day, so we set it up after our hearing to see if we could continue to operate our cycle shop. We went to court and were bombarded with dozens of neighbors. They told stories of our wild parties, reckless motorcycle riding, and our twenty-four-hour workdays. It wasn't enough to convince the counsel to kick us out. We were granted our variance and asked to leave before a riot broke out. We headed north to go hang out with the girls to celebrate. I believe that was the night it became official. I ended up dating my new tattoo artist. It was a match made in hell. We both liked drugs and alcohol. We both had enough of the games of dating, and her dad was tight friends with tough guys who didn't like me.

A few weeks later, I was working on an engine in the shop and kept hearing what sounded like a helicopter. I walked outside to see and, sure enough, hovering above our shop was a state police helicopter. Being paranoid, we hid our drugs and guns, then went home for the day. It was a good thing we did. The next morning, as I pulled into the shop, I couldn't help but notice all the police cars. Our neighbor ran out to meet me and said go, go, the cops got your partner. I was thinking about some of the cops episodes that I have watched and figured that wouldn't end good. So I walked in and got arrested. It turns out that they were looking for a stolen motorcycle that wasn't there (which means, no evidence, no arrest. Off with the cuffs, and we will shut the door behind you). We got blasted with cocaine after they left, but I think the adrenaline gave the drugs a run for the money.

After dodging those bullets, I found that settling down with my new girl was much more appealing. I spent less time at the shop and more time with her. It caused some issues in my business relationship and eventually that ended in yet again another ugly break up. One thing about the wild side is that nothing comes easy, and trouble is never too far away. I left the business and started working with my girlfriend at the tattoo shop as a piercer. A new town, a fresh start, but no less dysfunctional.

We started hanging out with some misfits from the area which got my evil mind churning. I decided to start a cult, well maybe not a cult but a group of people who would do our housework, simple chores, and bring business to the shop for the sense of belonging. It didn't take long to have a crowd, but it got pretty weird when one of the girls started hinting about getting rid of my girlfriend and taking her place. I will never forget that moment. I literally gathered everyone up, told them to get out, and that the experiment was over. It is crazy how things can go bad really quick.

Speaking of going bad really quick, we headed to a birthday party of one of my girlfriend's family members. It was a little kid, so I figured I would leave my .357 in my console of my Lincoln. After a few minutes of being there, my girlfriend's dad showed up. He invited me to step outside for a little conversation. When we got outside, he had one of his friends waiting to join us. He invited me in to his truck to go for a little ride. We went to his cabin by the river only a few minutes down the road. When we got there, I knew there was going to be trouble. I kept my back to a tree knowing that tough guys like to hit people from behind. Well, it turned into a little shove and slap with a warning to stop seeing his daughter or else. On the ride back to the party, he asked me if I had my gun, If I would have, this story would have a different ending.

When we got back, my girlfriend was pissed at her dad. We stood on a porch talking, and all I can remember is the thoughts of shoving him off the foot landing. We left right away, and as if I needed any motivation to marry this girl, that was it. We decided that it would be best to move away and start a new life in peace.

Without going into details, we went out with a bang. We headed up north to a town in the mountains called Emporium, where my first wife's relatives lived. We actually stayed with her uncle and his girlfriend for the first few days that we were there. Just like every other time that I had tried to move on to better things, it seemed that I was only sliding deeper in to the darkness. We may have left our enemies behind, but it didn't take long to make new ones.

We opened a tattoo shop in the center of town in a third-floor apartment. While some people objected, many people received us with open arms. Unfortunately, many of them were in the exact place we were trying to get out of. It didn't take long for us to be popping pills and trading work for drugs. One of the first days that we were there, we were on our way out of town to pick up supplies for the shop. It was late on a Friday night after just snorting some morphine and smoking some weed in our uninsured car when we came to a DUI checkpoint. My girlfriend was ready to turn around to avoid the stop, but that was a sure sign of guilt and a good way to get thoroughly checked out.

After arguing for a minute, we pulled up to the checkpoint and, lucky for us, a simple question of where are you headed and we're on our way. Business was good, and we were finding this place to be home, so we decided to get married. Not long after that, a local cocaine supplier approached me about dealing for him. The deal was too good to pass up, so I started my own little side business. I was back to not sleeping and partying with the wildest of the bunch. Fist fights, couples hooking up, and stuff being stolen was just a daily occurrence at our place. I got tired of dealing and was looking to upgrade our location, so I decided to burn my supplier. For those unaware of the term, I would ask for a larger than normal amount of drugs and then not pay for them. It all went down on Memorial Day weekend when my mother-in-law came to visit us. We were all messed up from the excessive amount of cocaine we were doing, but my mother-in-law was depressed about her living conditions. One of my buddies and I got the bright idea of taking off to Harrisburg to grab her son while she was sleeping, and bring him there so they could start a new life. In other words, kidnap him and hold them there against their will. It went as bad as to be expected. She woke up and figured out the plan, called her son, and told him to run. She threatened to call the police, so my wife held her at gunpoint until we got back.

After talking it out, things were smoothed over, and my wife drove her mom back home. After being home, her mom told the story to another family member which called probation on my wife. Oh yeah, I forget that detail. She was on probation. We got a call the very next day from her probation officer saying she needed a drug test within twenty-four hours. She convinced the officer to let her take it at our local courthouse which worked out good because she smuggled in some fresh urine we got from a client who was clean in exchange for a tattoo. After passing the test, her officer signed her off due to the fines being paid and her "good conduct."

Now that brings us to the visit from the supplier. He showed up that same day, looking for his two thousand dollars, and after notifying him that he wasn't getting it, there started a battle that would make things even more interesting. We took the money I made from selling the cocaine and moved into a street-level building directly across the street.

It made our business more accessible and our monkey business more noticeable. Word got around that I lost my supplier, so another one came around one day to see if I would sling for him. I did, and this time, we would add crack to the menu. As if I wasn't already messed up enough, the crack made me a paranoid angry heathen. Not a good mix. We started fighting a lot, and we got into other drugs like acid, special K, and mushrooms. I ended burning a side dealer on that stuff so that rodeo didn't last long. We had a woman who was meeting men at our shop to hook up with, so I worked up a deal to get a cut if she could use our back room to do business. My wife shut that down before it got started and ran the woman off at the same time. I started running to Pittsburgh and Buffalo to change up my suppliers for cocaine, and each place had their own dangers. We were burning the candle at both ends and walking into a powder keg. More trouble, more drugs, and I caught some charges that were thrown out by the judge for lack of a good case, and our stay there was coming to an end.

After making good with my wife's dad and having a special investigation running on us, we packed up shop and headed back to Harrisburg. The police weren't happy, but they picked up in our new place where they left off when we left. We decided to get clean and do things right this time, and to our credit, we made it about a month. That was long enough for the police to get bored watching us do nothing. We opened a new tattoo shop in Lemoyne, which is just across the river from Harrisburg. We got busy quick and decided to go out for a drink to celebrate. We walked in to the bar, and lo and behold, there was my old business partner from the cycle shop. I went up to the bar and ordered our drinks.

After pounding a handful of shots of Jack and throwing back a few Xanax, I decided to go talk to him. It went pretty well until everything got mixing up in my bloodstream. I was pretty wasted and could barely stand. Knocking over chairs and tables, they decided to lock me in the car until they got the place straightened up. That wasn't a good thing because I was smart enough to wind the window down and dive out in the parking lot. Yep, head first into a stone parking lot. I busted up my eye socket and tore deep gashes in my face. But that wasn't enough to stop me, so I headed back in to the bar. Just as I got to the door, someone opened the door and knocked me straight back on my head, split the back of my head open too. We ended up going to my old partner's shop where he superglued my head back together.

After a couple days in bed, I was good to go. We started hanging out again at either one of our places and, you guessed it, started moving cocaine again. This time, he had a few guys working with him, so we had some guys to run for us. One day, while at the tattoo shop, a young kid walked in looking for a job. He was a graffiti artist and wanted to tattoo. We really weren't looking for help, but he said he was living in a dumpster. I told him that if he could prove he lived in a dumpster, I would hire him. We left the shop and drove to a convenience store where his dumpster was. Sure enough, his stuff was set up in there. We grabbed his bags and went back to the shop. We started teaching him how to tattoo, and he fit right in with our drugs and mayhem.

A few of my wife's old girlfriends started coming around and hanging out. They added some estrogen to our little gang and even brought some drugs to the party. A couple others started to become regulars, hanging out and playing guitar and other forms of entertainment. We had a happening shop, which drew attention from a few tough guys from our past. This time, we had our own little gang, and it kind of escalated things. After an attempted robbery of our shop in which the kid we hired, shot at the guys, we decided to stock up our weapons. We had guns in every room, loaded and ready to go. We were unfit to have one gun, let alone several high capacity ones.

We got connected to a new cocaine supplier, two Guatemalan guys with reliable connections. One day, they dropped off a shipment at the tattoo shop. We headed back to the back room to make the transaction where I had a few of my closest associates hanging out. We had a tricked out AK-47 leaning up in the corner, loaded, and off safe. We all did a line and were standing there talking when one of the guys from Guatemala grabbed the AK and started pretending he was shooting at us. He didn't understand English, and I didn't understand Spanish, but by the looks on our faces, his brother knew the gun was loaded and ready to go. He stepped in front of him and pushed the barrel down. After a quick-underpants check, we laughed it off and went back to business. We had more close calls there than we did anywhere else. Life was going fast and coming to an end. The apartment upstairs opened up, so we moved the young kid in there. Being right along the main road through town kept things interesting. I used to love standing in front of the shop and watch the people go by. I remember looking down the street at a church that had a neon cross on the roof with Jesus Saves hanging underneath and laughing. If Jesus was saving anyone, it certainly wasn't any of us.

Someone dropped off a Bible and a prayer rug, well, a paper that resembled one with a picture of Jesus on it. I hung it up in our back room as a dartboard, and some friends would roll joints with the pages of the Bible. My wife's dad started coming around the shop, but I kept my eyes on him. We may have been getting along, but I didn't trust him at all. We had our moments. Little flare ups here and there, but I had bigger problems to stay on top of.

One night after work, the whole gang decided to go out for a drink near my buddy's cycle shop. My supplier wasn't picking up and were looking to party. I went outside of the bar to make a call, and a kid walked up to me and asked what I was looking for. I didn't answer him at first, but after leaving another message for my supplier, I took the bait. I told him some blow and asked him what he got. He showed me a gram and said fifty bucks. Being desperate I told him I would take it. I told him I had to get the money from my wife and just then one of my boys came by and was heading back to the shop. I handed him the cocaine and said we would be right there. The kid and I walked in to get the money and just when I handed it to him we were surrounded by undercover cops. I was busted in the act, but there was bad news. I didn't have the drugs! It was a set up, and it didn't work. The decoy dealer went over and spoke to one of the cops, and they let me go. We left out of there laughing, but I knew that someone was watching out for me.

My birthday that year was a defining moment in my relationship with my daughter. Earlier that morning, I went to the doctors to have my Xanax script renewed. I fed him a line that it wasn't working, and I needed it increased. He wrote me a script for the maximum dose that he could. Two milligrams, four times a day, which is sufficient for four people to forget what they did that day. I got the script filled and took a handful. We decided to close up shop for the day and party with our friends. We were trashed by noon when my dad called and said they had a cake and ice cream for me at the house. We actually lived with my parents to cut back on costs. They really put up with some stuff from me. We went back to the house around six for the cake and ice cream, but I was so high I could barely stay awake. I remember when my dad brought the cake out to sing. I literally passed out and fell on the floor. My wife said that they wanted to call an ambulance, but she kept telling them that I always did that. The sad thing was it was true.

Later that night, while I was passed out, my daughter tried to call me. She was in a car accident, and her mom was out of town. I never picked up the phone, and to this day, I know our relationship would be different if I could have.

I was getting really bad with the drugs and my anger. My wife's dad and I were back to fighting, and it was getting the best of me, and I was taking it out on her.

On October 4, a day after picking up my Xanax prescription and having a major blowout with my wife, I woke up with a note sitting on my chest. My wife had taken all but one of my two milligram Xanax, one hundred and eight to be exact. She said she was tired of living the way we were, and there was no hope for us to change. Her lifeless body laid beside me as I read the note. I jumped out of bed and ran to the kitchen to tell my parents that she overdosed. My dad wanted to call an ambulance, but I said we should just take her to the hospital ourselves. I was just angry and confused to the point that I couldn't think clearly. I had my dad turn around on the way to the hospital and said that I would rather take her myself. I ended up driving her to the tattoo shop instead. She had a pulse, so I figured I could just wake her up. I poured coffee down her throat, hoping to bring her around, but it wasn't working.

My old business partner came over and talked me into taking her to the hospital. We took her to the emergency room, and they had us bring her right into a room. I told them what she took, but they had to do bloodwork before they could help her. It was quick, but they found that it was just Xanax, so they gave her a shot of flumazenil to wake her up. I remember the scream she let out when she came to. It was an angry cry of reality to our life and how it felt to live it. They admitted her to the psych ward and told me that I could see her in the morning. My heart was crushed to pieces. I left the hospital and went to the tattoo shop and had the young kid tattoo a broken heart on my chest. When we were done, I went on a mission to go find enough drugs to kill the pain. The mission took me to one of the most dangerous parts of the city. I didn't care if I lived or died; I just wanted the pain to go away.

I encountered two dealers sitting outside of a playground, waiting for business. When I walked up to them, I pulled my gun out and told them I wanted drugs, a lot of them. They were pleading for their lives, so I handed them my gun. I said, "I will buy the drugs, or you could just kill me." They knew I was crazy and didn't want any trouble. They handed me the gun and walked me to an apartment. I told them the story of my wife overdosing, and they actually had sympathy for me. I hung out with them for a while then left with my stash. I did every single drug they gave me, and it didn't seem to dent the pain.

The next morning, I drove over to the hospital to see her. I put my gun in my glove box before driving to the parking garage. As I was headed to the front door of the hospital, I noticed a bunch of guys in suits standing by the door. As I walked passed them, they grabbed me and put me down on the sidewalk. My wife's dad got there before me and told them that I threatened to shoot him, and that I always had my gun on me. They took me into a room inside the door after finding no weapon on me. They asked for my side of the story which was exactly the way he told it. I really did want to kill him, just not right there or right then.

My brother was in the area so he decided to stop in the hospital to see if I was there visiting with my wife. He found out that they were holding me in a room to work things out and came to see me. He knew I was pissed off by what I was saying, so he told the nurse that I was a danger to myself. That was enough to get me put in a suicide watch room. Stripped down and pads on the walls, I sat there thinking about how much of a wreck my life was, but by no means was I thinking about suicide.

A doctor came in to see me and asked if I was on any drugs. I told him all of the drugs I did the night before. He thought I was lying, so they decided to draw blood for a screen. In the meantime, my brother called my dad to fill him in on what was going on, and it wasn't long before he was there too. They let him in the room to see me, and by the look on his face, I could tell it broke his heart. While we were talking, the doctor came back in with the results of my blood test. He looked at my dad and said, "I have good news and bad news. The good news is your son is honest. The bad news is that he has a drug problem with the amount of drugs and levels of each, some toxic."

I should not have been conscious, let alone driving to the hospital and holding a rational conversation. I really believe that God even protected me back then from death and damage to my brain and body.

A crisis counselor came in and interviewed me after that and decided that I was not suicidal and could be released. They gave me my clothes and release papers, and I was headed upstairs to see my wife. When I opened the door, the look on her dad's face was priceless. I told her that I would be back later and told him that our little issue wasn't over.

After a call to my doctor, I was able to get a replacement for my script and back in business. My wife was transferred to another hospital uptown to a psych ward for ten days. During one of the interviews, she told them that I was beating on her, but after an examination, it was clear that I wasn't hitting her. We fought, and I was verbally abusive, but I never hit her. Two days before she was released, I was on my way out of her door, and out from the elevator, stepped her dad and her aunts. He was drunk, and there was an audience, so he put on a show by calling me names and accusing me of trying to kill her. The nurses said we had to leave but I told them that I was on my way out, and that they could stay. I waited by his truck until he came out, and let's just say we exchanged some unfriendly words.

The night she was released was one of the hardest nights for me. I knew that nothing changed, but I had a feeling that she may try to kill herself again. But with all of my guns and drugs, I was afraid that the next time, she would be successful. We went on with life as usual, partying and arguing. One night, a friend of ours came in to the shop, wasted and out of his mind. He had some painkillers and wanted to share. We sat down and blew back a few, and he stumbled out the door to head home. The next morning, his girlfriend showed up bawling and yelling at us. After they went home, she fell asleep only to wake up to him dead sitting in his chair. She blamed me for his death and I understood, but it was his drugs, and we always partied. Nonetheless, he was dead.

My wife was messed up from the overdose already, but this pushed her paranoia over the edge. A couple days later, we headed in to work like any other day. We were only there maybe ten minutes when she started an argument over twenty dollars. I didn't remember anything about twenty dollars, and there was a reason I didn't. It was a distraction to get her out of the front door. She grabbed her tattoo machines and ran out the front door to the car of a waiting friend. They called the police and said that I tried to kill her. It wasn't long before the police showed up to question me. Luckily I had the young guy who worked for us there the whole time, and he testified to the same story of how it all went down. After they left, I got a call from one of her closest friends. Actually it was the one she lived with who introduced us a few years earlier for my tattoo. When I told her what went down, she came right over. She just had a baby but was partying like a rock star. She asked if we felt like partying so that's what we decided to do, have a going-away party for my wife.

I went down to the bank with a check I wrote from the business account which was in my wife's name. When I got to the bank, the teller went over to get the manager—never a good sign. He asked me when she wrote me the check, and I said just a little while ago. He said he would be right back. I didn't stick around to see what was going to happen next. I grabbed the check and headed out the door. I burnt that thing when I got to the shop. Good thing I did. A few minutes later, the cops showed up. Apparently she shut the bank account down after she left, and they knew I had forged the check. Again, no evidence, no crime. My wife's friend took a couple hundred bucks out of her account and off to partying we went.

All three of us headed out to the bars in Downtown Harrisburg to look for some drugs. We ran into a few gang members from "the hill," a rough section of the city. We got to talking, and they asked if we would tattoo their gang sign on them. We made a deal, if they got us some crack, then we would set them up to do the tats. They had it on them, and we set them up for six o'clock the next evening. We hung out for a bit then went back to the shop to get cracked out. The next day, we were getting the shop ready for business. I was running the sterilizer and setting up a station for myself to tattoo. The young man we had working for us was working hard at his drawing station all day. I asked him what he was working on. He said some new drawings.

I went about my business to set up for our evening appointments. As the time drew near, I took my gun out of my pants and put it in the cabinet above my station. Anytime I tattooed, I would take it out to avoid static electricity causing it to blow a hole in my leg. I went to the back room to get our equipment out of the sterilizer for our appointments. When I came to the front of the shop, it was six o'clock, and our boys from the city were just pulling up. The young man looked at me and said, "We got this. I am going to be here with you forever." They came in the door, and we started talking details of price and design. We already knew, but they let us know that if any other gangs found out, they would come after us. We weren't concerned about any of that. The young man working with me said he wasn't up to tattooing at the moment and said he needed to go upstairs for a minute. Unsure of what was going on, the guys started offering more money or drugs for the tattoos. He said it wasn't that; he would be right back. He walked out the front door and *bang*. A loud shot rang through the shop. He stuck the gun to his head and shot himself. He was dead instantly. The gang members ran out of the shop and sped off toward the city. His girlfriend was upstairs at his apartment and heard the shot. She came down the stairs and saw him lying there.

She cried out that she didn't want to live anymore, so I took the gun out of his hand and out of her reach. Two young girls walked by the shop and asked what happened. I told them to keep going and to get away. It was not a pretty sight to see, and to a teenage girl, it was horrific. The police came from every direction. I had the gun which did not look good. They had me put the gun down and asked me why I shot him. I told them that he shot himself, but with my witnesses gone, that story wasn't working. I was put in handcuffs and sat on a couch until they could get the scene secure. Meanwhile, breaking news came over the six o'clock news about a homicide on the eight hundred block of Market Street, the news my parents were watching.

Knowing that it was my shop, my dad headed over to see what was going on. As the detectives were searching for evidence, they found a suicide note on his drawing station. They immediately took the handcuffs off and called crisis intervention. They asked me why I had the gun, and I told them the story of his girlfriend not wanting to live. They believe that may have saved her life that night. The street was blocked off in both directions for several blocks. My dad had a cop bring him to the shop from down the road. I will never forget the elated look on my dad's face when he saw me sitting on the couch. I stood up and hugged him for what seemed to be an hour. The police were looking for an address for his parents but couldn't find one.

They asked if he lived upstairs and if they could look there. After they headed up, I looked at my dad and said it was about to get worse. He was growing marijuana in one of the rooms, and my name was on the lease. After finding what they needed, the cops came down and asked me whose apartment it was. I told them it was in my name, but he lived there. After a brief discussion among themselves, they offered me this deal—go pull the plants and put them in a bag, shut the shop down and get out of their town, and they would pretend it never happened. Upstairs I went with Dad picking pot plants. When everything was said and done there, the coroner gave me his card and said they were off to notify the parents. If they were to stop or call before he got to them, I was supposed to call him. A couple minutes later, his dad walked in the door. He said, "Where is my son?"

I told him that I needed to make a phone call first. He came over to the phone and said it again. I looked him in the eye and told him that he shot himself tonight and was dead. I will never forget the agonizing cry that came from the man as he fell to the floor. Many things happened that day, but the one thing that still sticks with is the paragraph written to me in the suicide note. He said that I was better than what my life was, and that I should get off of drugs and do something good with my life. This is why the title to the book is *Eleven Two Seven*, the date this young man took his own life.

However, I didn't take his advice. I moved in with my wife's friend after she kicked her baby's dad out, and I drank my pain away, although it never really went away. I started working with my brother the following Monday after the shop shut down to keep my bills paid and pass the time. I ended up leaving that girl a month later because I was too broken to try to have a normal life with a baby and all the drama that came with it. I ended up staying at a younger girl's apartment. She would hang out at the tattoo shop and play guitar while we would smoke weed. It wasn't my intention to make anything permanent out of it, but we ended up dating. I was still a mess.

One night, after drinking my paycheck away at a local bar, I decided to head over to my old shop. To this day, I recognize several miracles happened that night. The first was that I made it to the shop without killing anyone. I was blind drunk to the point of running into the pole in front of the shop with my car. I was drunk, depressed, and desperate. I lost my wife, my money, my shop, my relationship with my daughter, visitation rights for my son, and the little sanity that I had left. I got out of the car and dialed up my wife's phone. Her friend answered and was everything but understanding with me. I told her to tell my wife not to worry about filing for divorce because I was going to kill myself. She said good and hung up. I took my gun out of my pants, the same gun that the young man used to kill himself and put it to my head. With tears of pain running down my face, I pulled back the hammer and *bang*. I woke up in my girlfriend's apartment. It wasn't a dream but another miracle of God's grace.

Apparently I passed out before I pulled the trigger. One of the neighbors whom I used to talk to was walking his dog and found me lying on the sidewalk with the gun in my hand, finger on the trigger, and the hammer still back. As he walked up to me, the phone in my jacket pocket was ringing. He grabbed the phone and answered it. It was my girlfriend. He told her about my situation and my car, so she came right over to get me. She called my dad and my friend to come help her get my car out of there and deal with me when I woke up.

It wasn't pretty. I was threatening to punch everyone and threw myself down a full set of steps. Battered, bruised, broken, but still alive, my dad took me to their house to sleep it off. I don't know how she ever put up with me, but she did. I would take money out of her jeans and buy crack and pills and would get drunk, and she would have to drive me from the bars that would kick me out. We would fight occasionally but never anything too serious. We moved around a couple times looking for a fresh start, but we kept showing up.

In March 2009, we were living in Carlisle, Pennsylvania, and working at a salon. She did nails, and I was doing tattoos and makeup. I injured my back but didn't have the money to miss work, so I was on prescription pain pills, buying and trading them for other more potent drugs and still drinking.

I ended up not feeling real well one night and ended up in the emergency room. I remember the TV show on the television in my room was *Davey and Goliath*. The show where they got stuck on a freight train after playing on it while it was parked. The sound of the train as saying, "Alone, alone, alone," but Goliath reminded Davey that with God, we are never alone. It seems stupid to put this in my story, but it is quite significant in the next few days. After a CT scan, they determined that my Crohn's disease was full-blown again. The believed I was going to need surgery, but the specialist was out of town that week. They gave me steroids and sent me home with an appointment with him on the day of his return. I was in so much physical pain that I didn't have room for the emotional pain. A couple days went by, and I was home on the couch with some extra pain meds that a buddy of mine dropped off. I remember lying there in the silence of midday, going in and out of what felt like sleep.

In the depth of what I believe was my spirit, I heard a voice. That voice said, "I have a plan for your life, and you have done everything you could to avoid me." The voice spoke of healing me and giving me a new life. My end of the deal was to live that new life and share this story with everyone. I wanted healed but didn't want to change. Filled with pride, I somehow believed that whatever this voice that I was hearing would fall victim to my manipulation. I half-heartedly agreed as if my fingers were crossed. At the very second that thought came to my head, it felt like

I was crushed by the weight of the world, and in a sense, I was. As my body was emptied of its waste and breath, I remember thinking that I lied to this voice in my head, and it killed me. Feeling deep remorse, I plead for my life with the understanding that Jesus Himself had given me a second chance at life. With that, I awoke, covered in urine and lying in my feces, feeling as if I had stepped into a whole new world. I had a new energy. My pain was gone, and there I knew that the living God had touched me.

Within minutes, my girlfriend came home to find me vacuuming the living room and cleaning up my mess. I told her the story, and she called her parents who were Christians. We headed to my parents to tell them what happened, and I remember my mom's tears of joy at my fresh encounter with Jesus. That Sunday, we went to a church in Duncannon, Pennsylvania. As the worship team played "He touched me," the pastor got up and said that someone named Daniel had a story to tell. I stood up in tears and made my way to the front of the church. I shared my story with the congregation, and we all praised God. After the service, the pastor asked me to come to his office. He gave me a Bible and asked if I would be interested in being a disciple. I agreed, and we began meeting at his office and house to study the Bible. We began to tell our customers at the salon about the goodness of God and what Jesus did for me. My follow-up appointment with my doctor confirmed that my body was alive and well. Things were going better than ever before in my life. But the owner of the shop had asked us to stop talking about God. We felt a conviction about the request and decided to leave the salon.

We began working for my girlfriend's dad's excavating business, sharing with everyone my encounter with Jesus. I was learning a lot and hearing from the Lord daily.

My relationship with my daughter was dissolved, but her high school graduation was coming up, and I couldn't wait to tell her the news. That day arrived, and we decided to go. My dad suggested that I should get her flowers like the rest of the parents. I had a check in my spirit as if that was a bad idea, so we didn't stop and grab any. As the graduation was happening, I went down into the hallway where she would be exiting the arena to wait for her. After the graduation, she came into the hallway with the other kids. So I congratulated her and reached out to give her a hug. When she saw me, she turned around and ran across the arena floor away from me. My heart was broken, and my mind was confused. How could that happen? God had been so good to me. Why would He fail me now?

To be honest, I was struggling for a few days after that. Then one night, we were sitting around, watching the Gospel of John on television. As we were watching, I heard the Lord in my spirit reveal that He allowed me to go through that episode with my daughter to have a better understanding of how it hurts Him when His children turn from Him. Even as I sit here writing this, I know there were many lessons that night, including a little glimpse into the pain I caused my daughter when I left. I couldn't change the past, but I was trusting that God would change the future. I was spending more time with my son and spending even more time around the church. I was working the soundboard, helping with Bible studies, and anything else

I could get my hands on. My girlfriend and I ended up getting engaged, and all was right with my world.

One day, we were driving home, and an old friend popped into my head. I blurted his nickname out loud, and my girlfriend thought I was crazy. I told her about him and some of the stuff he would do. Later that night, we were watching television with her parents, and we saw a medical helicopter coming across the fields and looking to land. It was a rural area, so that wasn't a frequent occurrence. We jumped in the truck and headed down the road toward the landing zone. When we got to the fire police directing traffic, her dad asked what was going on. He couldn't say, but we knew it wasn't good. Her dad owned another property down the road, so he told them he wanted to go check it out and make sure everything was okay. They let us through, and when we got to the property, we saw the police and the ambulance across the street at the neighbors. Her dad said their last name, and immediately it hit me, it was my old friend's last name. Sure enough it was the friend who came to mind earlier that day. He attempted suicide but didn't die. He was flown to the hospital with a gunshot wound to his head. He lived and eventually recovered. I couldn't believe that God would remind me of him just hours before this tragedy. I have come to learn to pray for those that come to mind. I had many similar encounters with words of knowledge like that. I must have been hard to live with because my girlfriend became hurtful and began trying to control me.

We decided to take a trip to Emporium so that I could share my testimony with those who knew how bad I was when I lived there with my ex-wife. It was my birthday weekend, so we were going to make a time of it. On our way there, my blazer began to blow white smoke out of the exhaust. That's usually not a good sign. We just made it up Seven Mountains when we decided to pull into a campground to see what was going on. I checked everything I could but didn't find anything obviously wrong with it. We decided to get a spot and camp there for the night.

The next morning, I started up the blazer, and the smoke had stopped. We decided it was too risky to go any farther north, so we figured we would stay there for the weekend. We went to the office to see what there was to do in the area. We found a local church directory along with some pamphlets and went back to our site. We set our plans to go fishing and grab dinner that night, then hit a local church in the morning before going home. I picked a local church that night, then used the rest of the directory to start our campfire. The next morning, as we were getting ready for church, I felt the Lord say not to go to that church. I told my girlfriend, and she agreed. I asked the Lord where we should go and felt that I should turn the page over. There was another church on the back, so we headed there.

When we walked in the place, it was filled with older people in suits and dresses. We stuck out like a sore thumb. We sat down toward the back, and a woman came over to us right away. She asked if we were just visiting or looking for a church to join. We told her the story, and she walked away like she saw a ghost. The worship team started, and the service was underway. I wasn't sure what was going on, but I had a feeling something was happening. After worship, the lady who spoke to us went to the front. She was very emotional as she began to speak. She said that her husband, who happened to be the pastor, received a call that morning from another church asking if he could fill in for their pastor due to a family emergency. After praying, they decided he should go, which left them without a sermon. She said she was just planning to discuss some of the issues the church was facing and have the congregation pray over them. She then told the story of her talking to us after we sat down and then asked if I would come up front. When I got up front, she asked me to tell the story of how we got there, then share my testimony to the congregation. So I did just that. As I spoke, the older men in the church were tearing up, and some of the women were crying. I couldn't understand what was going on, but I knew it was God. As I was drawing near the end of my testimony, the woman came through the back door of the church with her husband.

When I finished, they came up front with me. The pastor was clearly shaken as he addressed the congregation. He said to me, "What you don't know is that our church has been struggling for a while, and a couple of weeks ago, we prayed as a church that if God wanted us to continue on, he would have to send us a sign. Someone who was definitely not like us would have to bring the message if we should close or not."

That blew me away when he said that, and I could tell I was in the middle of one of many sovereign setups. He asked if would pray over the congregation, and of course I said yes. What I didn't know is that he meant each one of them. For what felt like hours, I prayed over each one of the congregation. Afterward they asked if they could take us out to lunch, so we went with them and had a great time of fellowship. The church is still around today nearly ten years after that crazy encounter. If you are wondering about the blazer, it went on to run fine for another two years.

Things were surreal, and most of the time, they were great. Something was changing though. People around me were becoming hateful and jealous. My fiancé would continue to bring up the fact that I was a mess when we got together and a drug addict. People in the church became judgmental. One day, I was meeting with my pastor for discipleship and prayer. It was a great time in the Lord's presence. As we were praying, the Holy Spirit revealed to me that a long-time promise to prayer was being released over the pastor and his wife. I remember the moment as if it was yesterday. I told him what I heard, and we rejoiced in tears. The next day, I got a call from another pastor at that church. He asked if I could swing by to see him. When I got there, he told me that my words were out of line. That I could be responsible for the failing of our pastor's faith when the miracle doesn't happen. I knew it was the Lord speaking to me, but I was confused why it was a bad thing to share such great news. I received the correction and left. To be honest, I was beginning to question why God would be so awesome, yet His people were so cruel. I was hurt by the closest to me and the ones who should have known better. Things continued to get worse both at home and at church, and all I could do was pray that God would make changes. And he did. After some misunderstandings, I broke off the engagement with my fiancé, which was good for me but brought even more judgment by the church. I ended up back at my parent's house again, but this time, it wasn't because of drugs or anything too crazy. I continued to meet with the pastor and be a disciple.

I was doing my laundry one day and met this woman at the laundry mat. I shared my testimony with her and another guy who was there. It turned out that she was the owner, and I ended up dating her. We hit it off really well, and my son became good friends with her daughter. She was as broken as I was, and we enjoyed church and began to start building a life together. We would go out to dinner and have a few beers which wasn't a good idea for me. She was on nerve medication which before too long, I would ask for one and snort it. The church was still judgmental. I was hurt and heading back to some of my old habits. Before too long, insecurities returned, and our relationship became rocky at best. I drank more and began to do more drugs. I started a new job which was extremely physical which got me using pain medicine again. And just like that, I quit going to church and began to regress to my old ways. I met a woman at work who knew me from several years ago, and we hit it off. She was married, but like before, that didn't stop me. We got close and ended up having an affair. It went on for a while as my relationship with my girlfriend continued to struggle. One day at work, I got a text from my girlfriend calling me out on my affair. She had copies of all of our text messages. And just like that, I was back at my parents' house again because of my stupid decisions. I continued in the affair and ended up getting my own place along the river in Harrisburg. A member of her family found out about our affair and tried to run me over with a truck. Eventually her husband found out, and we broke it off.

I was back to doing cocaine, heroin, and drinking excessively. I went to drop my rent check off one day at the property management company that handled my apartment. There was a pretty woman working there at the front desk, so of course, I would strike up some conversation. It was casual at first as I had enough going on juggling my job, addictions, and a few other girls whom I would date once in a while. I got injured at work a few times but couldn't report it because I would fail the mandated drug test. So I would up the pain medicine and work through it. Eventually I made my move on the woman at the property management company, and through work-related circumstances, we ended up in a bar with a friend of hers, and we hit it off. That's when she told me she was married. Again, that never stopped me before, so I was again in another affair.

It didn't last long because she became guilty of her double life. We broke it off which sent me in to an even faster downward spiral. I was buying heroin off the streets, drinking heavily, and as I tell everyone, I am probably the only person who would pray over their heroin. I knew God was real, but I also knew that I walked away from Him. He never gave up on me though.

One day, coming home from my morning shift at work with barely enough gas to get me to work in the afternoon and no money until pay day, I was walking to the steps of my apartment. A young man came up to me and asked me about a building that was being redone on my block. I told him that I had no idea what was going on. He told me that it used to be a Christian-run rehab/halfway house. He said that he witnessed many drug addicts encounter Christ and watched their life change right before his very eyes. I felt a deep conviction come over me. He said, "I won't take up any more of your time," and started to walk away. As I turned to walk up my stairs, he said, "Wait a minute." He walked back to me and put out his hand. He said, "God told me you need this," and handed me a fifty-dollar bill. I thanked him, and he went on his way. How could God provide for an adulterer like me? Why hasn't He given up or struck me dead yet? I am making a mess of my little world and taking people down with me.

That Saturday, I went and grabbed some heroin and a six pack and decided to spend the day inside getting wasted and listening to music. By late afternoon, I could barely keep my eyes open, so I laid down for a nap. Not sure how long I was out for, but I woke up to the sound of many boots running up the steps. Coming from a criminal background, I can tell you that isn't a good sound. I no sooner sat up, and there was a pounding on my door with the call, "Open up, it's the Harrisburg police department!"

I walked over to the door and looked out the peephole. Sure enough I had a hallway filled with cops. As I opened the door, they rushed in with guns drawn asking where the body was. Having no idea what they were talking about, I said feel free to search my apartment, but I have no idea what body they were talking about. After searching my place and finding no one, they said there was a trail of blood leading from the sidewalk out front the whole way to my door. Being a maintenance man for the property, I had keys to every apartment. I opened the neighbor's apartment, and on his floor was a bloody knife and bloody jeans. Apparently he was juggling knives on the sidewalk and cut the main artery in his leg. He called his social worker who took him to the hospital. How is God in this? Well, while searching my apartment, the police overlooked the bags of heroin sitting on my kitchen counter. I believe to this day God hid them in plain view to keep me from charges. I had a sense that things were getting too close for comfort but was totally unable to get free on my own.

I dropped my rent check off at the office and saw the woman whom I had the affair with. She had lost a considerable amount of weight, and I was looking pretty rough myself. We decided to meet for lunch later that day to discuss what has been going on in our lives since the breakup. At the lunch, she shared that her guilt had brought her to a place of complete separation in her already damaged marriage, and I shared that my drug use had increased and how God was appearing in crazy ways. She said that she was planning on leaving her husband later but wasn't sure how or when. I headed off to work, and she went about her day.

Later on, while I was at work, I got a text from her saying she left a note for her husband and was at my apartment. She already had a key being a property manager. Part of me was happy because I knew I needed someone around me to get me out of my outrageous lifestyle, but another part of me knew this was just another slap to the face of God. She moved in with me and it was far from a honeymoon. Everyone was against us but my family. We drank every night, and I couldn't quit the heroin. We fought constantly and were broken to pieces. She got a settlement from her divorce, and we decided to open a tattoo shop with the money. I quit my job and started working on that venture. It didn't take us long to get it up and running. We hired an artist who grew up as a neighbor to my first wife and I early on in our marriage. She was just beginning in the tattoo business but was willing to learn. She became like a daughter to us with all of the time we spent together.

We hired a few other artists who came and went, but we just couldn't seem to get the business to grow. Maybe it was my reputation or maybe it was God pushing us somewhere else? Sure enough we were getting behind on our bills and needed to make some quick cash. I put a post on social media, asking if anyone in Emporium would be interested in getting a tattoo or piercing. If enough people would respond, we would go up there and have a tattoo weekend. That was where my second wife and I had a tattoo shop years before. The response was great, so we set our sights to head to Emporium for a tattoo weekend. Now I left that town earlier due to the heat the police were putting on me and my wife, so I wasn't sure how it was going to go, but something told me to go anyway. We headed up north with two cars filled with tattoo supplies. We weren't there twenty minutes before one of the local police started to inquire about why I was there. We set up shop at a buddy's house to do business. It was a success between our artist and myself; we made nearly a thousand dollars, which was good but not enough to keep us running back home. After we got home and back to the shop, we were sitting around, talking, and my girlfriend said she really liked Emporium, so we should move there. It may have been the drugs or maybe just my craziness, but it sounded like a great idea. There was a job fair the following Monday for a factory in Emporium. We decided that we would go apply and try to find an apartment while we were there. We headed up that Monday morning and went straight to the job fair. We applied then went to look for an apartment. It was no surprise that we were turned down by every last one we inquired about. After all, my reputation there was not good at all. We stayed at a local motel that night and figured we would try again the next day. I got a call from the factory, saying that I was hired, which was great to have when we would look for apartments that day. We went to a local café for breakfast, and the owner waited on us.

We told her our situation, and she hired my girlfriend on the spot. Now all we needed was a place to live. After striking out a couple more times, I said if only we could run into my old landlord. Although I owed him money and left on a bad note, he was a Christian, and I was sure he would give us a chance. We pulled over in front of my old tattoo shop, which was now vacant, and contemplated how we could reach him. My girlfriend said we need to pray that we see him. What? She wanted to pray?

Anyhow we said a little prayer which I interrupted and sat there for a couple minutes. I got a message from a girl whom I tattooed, saying her tattoo may have been infected.

I told her that we were in town and would swing by to look at it. She gave me her address, and we headed out to see her. As we pulled up to her place, there was a pickup in the road being unloaded of some building supplies. Sure enough, it was my old landlord. I jumped out of the car and walked over to him. He gave me a hug and asked what I was doing there. I told him our situation and introduced him to my girlfriend. He said that my old shop was open, and there was a room that could easily become a bedroom. We headed over there to look and work things out. We made the deal. We were going to live there and tattoo part time on my days off. We headed back to Harrisburg to get things wrapped up and to pack and begin our new life. And oh, what a new life it was, on the road with a rental truck full of stuff, a car with two dogs, and seven dollars to our name. When we got there, our landlord had a few guys there to help us unload. It was a big help because we were exhausted from all of the running. We got set up, including the tattoo equipment that day, and ate with the help of some old friends of mine. The next day, we put the open sign on to see if we could make a few bucks to get groceries and stuff for work. We ended up making over $300 that day and decided that I would just tattoo instead of work at the factory. We were under the watchful eye of the police, the community, and my landlord's wife. She was skeptical of any change that I may have gone through and rightly so. My life was a mess at the moment, but this time around, I knew that God was capable of turning it around.

We had to give our car back to the bank because we couldn't afford the high payment. Our landlord told us we could park it in one of his partner's lots until the bank came to pick it up. One of the tenants called the police, so they showed up at our door. One of the officers was being a jerk and asking me why I left the last time and what happened to my ex-wife. The other officer was cool and told the officer who was questioning me that they had the answer to why the car was parked there, and that they should go. I knew it was going to be a challenge but no idea how much of one. The drugs all but stopped, and the drinking was only occasional. We had too much going on and too many eyes watching to be living a crazy life. We still had our problems. Believe me, it was not easy living.

Our landlord came in to the shop one day and made us a deal. He would get a tattoo if we visited his church. We didn't jump right on it, but we eventually caved in. I will never forget the first time. The officer who was at our shop earlier, the cool one, was there. The old judge whom I stood before was there. And a bunch of people who tried their hardest to accept us were too. I did have a guy explain to me what a B-I-B-L-E was, emphasis added to reflect the level of intelligence he assumed I had. With all of that being said, it wasn't half bad. He didn't take up his end of the deal, but it didn't stop us from trying.

We started to go to the church weekly, sometimes after a Saturday night of drinking. It was good. There were times of conviction, times of humor, but most of all, fellowship with others in the community. One Sunday, after church, our landlords showed up and invited us to a picnic. We weren't too sure, but they were insistent. So we hopped in their truck and headed off...to the judge's house. Yes, the judge whom I stood in front of a few times before. It wasn't really a picnic either; it was a small group cookout Bible study. Talk about uncomfortable! It was tense when we got there to say the least. But after a while, we were all sitting around, eating, and the judge decided to open up. He asked me what my story was. After I told him everything that I had been through, he decided to open his own heart. He said that when he heard I moved back to Emporium, his first thought was *oh no*. He even contacted the new judge to be on the lookout for my name and, if possible, get me out of town. But after seeing me at church and out in the community volunteering, he knew he had made a mistake. He was one of the first Christians who was actually real and transparent to me. It was a divine appointment and a clear defining moment in my restoration to Jesus.

We continued to fellowship at church and with our small group so much that they became our family. One day, Shana came up to me and said she was feeling convicted about being married. Now I had asked her several times to marry me, but she said no. Not because she didn't want to, but marriage was a failure for us in the past, and she didn't want to risk it.

Besides we had some junk in our lives that had to go. After keeping her hanging, I finally said yes. We asked our pastor that Sunday if we could talk at some point that week.

After applying for our marriage license, he came over a couple of days later, and we asked if he would marry us. By the look on his face, I could tell that we were about to get shot in the chest by that religious spirit again. Our church had a policy that they wouldn't marry anyone who lived together, no exceptions. I understood the first part, but the no exceptions part, I wasn't too fond of. After giving us some crazy options and my temper flaring, we told him that we would get back to him.

We were hurt, but we knew that God was calling us to get married. That Friday, we went to the district justice and made it official. Our landlords showed up with flowers, and we went out for lunch afterward. That Sunday, I had a peace come over me at church that was unable to be described. (Yes, we still went to that church.) Later that night, my wife described the same feeling. It was clear that God was breaking through to our wounded hearts, and He was definitely up to something. That Monday afternoon, our pastor called to see if we had made a decision about making the changes we needed to make to get married in the church. I told him how we went to the district justice the Friday before and how we had peace just a day ago in the church. We ended our conversation and went about our business. A few minutes later, he called back and asked if we would be there for a little while. If I'm honest, I reluctantly said yes. I was still hurt by the no exception rule the church had put in place. After all, we wanted to get married to honor God out of conviction for our living in sin. When he showed up, he had brought us gift cards to buy ourselves wedding rings. We cried and, of course, received them as an act of kindness. We continued to go to that church and spend most of our time with our small group.

A couple of weeks later, I had a dentist appointment to get a referral to have most of my bad teeth removed. Smoking crack, doing meth, and getting punched in the mouth will put a hurtin' on your teeth. When I got to the dentist, they decided to clean my teeth and suggested to fix them instead. Well, whatever they were using made me sick to my stomach. By the time I got home, I was vomiting. I felt like a train ran me over. After a few hours of that, we decided to go to the emergency room as it seemed to be some kind of allergic reaction. They gave me some meds to calm my stomach down and sent me home. I continued to vomit off and on. I got up in the middle of the night to go to the bathroom, and when I did, it was pure blood. Now having had Crohn's disease, I wasn't as alarmed as most people would be with that amount of blood. I showed my wife and said if it was still like that in the morning, we would go back to the hospital. When I got up, it was actually worse. We got ready and headed to the hospital. Right as we walked in the hospital, I had to use the bathroom again, and the amount of blood was increasing. By the time I got to the triage nurse, I had five of these bowel movements of solid blood. At first, they didn't believe me when I told them how much blood I had been passing, but they put what they call a hat in the toilet to measure the blood. Within minutes, I filled the hat plus made a mess of the floor. The emergency room was in panic mode. My room was filled with nurses, doctors, and even a surgeon. I was hemorrhaging and needed treatment immediately. I was taken upstairs after several IVs were put in with meds to help clot the blood. After checking my hemoglobin that evening, they believed I needed a blood transfusion. They wouldn't let my wife stay with me that night, and some strange stuff happened. My room phone could call everyone but her. They started my first transfusion, so I called my landlord to have her call me. I was mostly peaceful, but there were times of fear that would creep in. They told me that if the bleeding didn't stop in twenty-four hours, I would be taking a helicopter ride to Pittsburgh for more detailed treatment.

Something inside me knew that it would as I told them confidently that it would stop by then. It did, but I was not out of the woods yet. My blood was low and still hadn't had anything to eat or drink. A nasty thunderstorm came through and knocked the electricity out at the hospital. The backup system was limited but sufficient to run my monitors and IV machines. When the power came back on, the fire alarm went off in the hospital. Convinced it was the power outage, the nurses shut the room doors and told us there was nothing to worry about.

My wife jokingly asked what we would do if the hospital was really on fire. I told her that we would make a rope from the sheets and go out the window. She walked over to open the curtains to see how far it would be, and right outside my window was thick black smoke. We could see firetrucks heading to the fire. Apparently the backup generator caught some building supplies on fire when it kicked on. It was put out, and I was eating and drinking without any signs of blood. They gave me another transfusion to get my blood up before they discharged me. The doctor said I was lucky. At one time, my hemoglobin was half gone. They couldn't understand how it was possible for me to be walking and talking with half of my blood missing.

My wife and I knew that God had manifested His presence with us for those three days.

After coming home, we were outside smoking cigarettes when I watched a couple drug deals go down. I asked God what I could do to stop the madness that ran wild in that town. Within seconds, I found myself in a vision at a place called the Lookout. It was a place that overlooked the town from a mountain on the south side. I was standing with a group of people praying. I felt the Lord say, "Go to the mountain and pray. Take the churches with you and pray," and He would do the rest. After telling an elder from our small group about the vision, we set our hearts to meet there that Sunday evening and begin what would be four faithful years of praying over that community. As soon as we started meeting there for prayer, there was a visible difference in the community. At first, the difference was so bad that a local police officer went to our pastor and told him we needed to stop praying because crime had increased to the point that they needed additional officers.

Biblically we knew that we were on the right path because everywhere that Jesus would show up, some form of evil would stir. This went on for a few more weeks, and we felt like the Lord telling us to launch the ministry that He called me to three years earlier. Our landlord had a building open up in town and put us up in there. I was meeting with our pastor every Monday morning for accountability and to discuss how the ministry would take shape. Our small group became our board along with our pastor, and on a Monday night in September 2012, Painted Soldier Ministry was born. I remember my first sermon there as if it were yesterday. I started off standing in a cardboard box as a reference to how we try to keep God in a box. I stepped out of the box and kicked it out of the door of our meeting room. It felt natural to be preaching, effortless, as if it was what I was called to do. God moved powerfully right from the start. People got saved, people got healed, and people got offended. Not just those whom I was preaching to but those in some of the local churches.

One church was accusing me of being a false prophet because we owned a tattoo shop. Another said that we were starting a cult. None of that really bothered me nor my wife at first. We were happy to be out of our dysfunctional lifestyle and to be hearing from God and being in His presence. God continued His work in our lives and marriage. We got free from everything but cigarettes, which I believe was because we weren't ready to give them up. The local paper did an article about our prayer on the mountain and about our local outreach. Those who were for us were coming alongside of us with encouragement and whatever support they could give. On the other hand, those that were against us began to show up at our shop and outreach and ask us questions like, "How can you sleep at night knowing you are sending people to hell?" I wasn't sure how I was sending people to hell, and besides that, I slept like a rock. Another woman came to our outreach and said that my testimony didn't add up, and that I was going to hell for being a false teacher.

There was a common denominator in these persecutions, and it was the church they attended. So my wife and I decided to go to the source of this nonsense and get to the bottom of it. We went to the church to talk to their pastor. We had a good conversation. He was honest and told us that our tattooing had demonic roots, and if the Holy Spirit was leading us, we would know that. Our reply was simply, "Why wouldn't you pray for us instead of praying against us." Well, he did pray for us to get a new source of income and for us to see a deeper truth. We were grateful, and that brought any direct attacks from that congregation to a halt. However, the attacks were far from over. While praying at the Lookout on a Sunday, I ended up with a tick bite. Thinking nothing of it, we just removed it and went about our business. That tick bite soon turned into joint pain, headaches, and lack of energy that soon had me on the sidelines for tattooing.

In the meantime, many of the local pastors had been criticizing our ministry and failing to recognize us as a legitimate ministry. I probably had a lot to do with it. I recognized the failure in the local church and didn't keep that opinion from them. I was a guest at one of the ministerial association meetings and spoke of the lack of power the church had in our community. I believe my charge to them was "playing church." I was asked why I didn't seek their approval to do ministry in the town. I was simply being obedient to God's call, and besides that, I wasn't aware that the church had such a rule similar to territorial motorcycle clubs. What I did know was this, people were responding to the spirit of God at our meetings, something I didn't see when attending local churches. I ended up at the doctor's several times for my aches and pains, but they ended up sending me to physical therapy. My body hurt, but my spirit was more alive than ever.

One day, while we were standing in front of the tattoo shop, a woman came up to me and asked to buy a gift certificate. Not feeling any better, I told her that I wasn't sure if I would be tattooing again due to my body feeling so bad. She said to me, "You have to... God told me that you are the only one to reach my husband."

Intrigued, I asked her who her husband was, and it ended up being an old friend of mine from the last time I was in town. He was a veteran with a good heart. He loved his beer and cussed like the sailor he was. I sold her the gift certificate and told her that I would let her know when I was able to tattoo again. During this time, our landlord stopped in and told us that the cycle shop in town closed down. He had an interest in that business as an investor. Knowing my past motorcycle experience, he asked if we would be interested in changing careers.

After prayer and not knowing if I would recover enough to tattoo again, we decided to go in to the cycle business. As we were working on transitioning for one business to the other, I ended up getting diagnosed with Lyme disease, which was a relief because the with the proper treatment, I was starting to feel better. It seemed that God was working harder when I was barely able to get out of bed. The ministry was flourishing, and people were noticing. We were making a dent in the addiction crises with the power of Jesus, and the crowds were growing. After a few conversations with my old veteran friend, I decided to give him the money back for the gift certificate his wife bought for him. But he flat-out refused and said that he would wait until I had the time. We launched our motorcycle shop just before spring that year. It started pretty quick with the work piling up to the point of having to hire additional employees. As much as I love motorcycles, my heart was in ministry which made me despise running the shop. God used it though for many things.

I was working on a motorcycle one morning, and our pastor came in to talk to me. He and one of the elders had a leading to ask me to help out with the baptisms coming up that weekend. A few of the people from our outreach were getting baptized along with other members of the church. I was honored to be a part of such a special day. A few hours later, an acquaintance from town came in to the shop. He told me that God was mad that I sold some of my tattoo equipment. He said that God told him that I was supposed to destroy it so nobody could use it to steal the souls of those getting tattooed. I knew it wasn't God but just another opinionated believer trying to convict me of my sins. I about had it with tattooing and the trouble it was causing. So I set up my last appointment with my old Navy buddy.

That weekend, the baptisms went great, so great that they stirred the hearts of the religious folks enough to tell the pastor that I contaminated the baptismal, and that the baptisms didn't count. That week, I finally got to tattoo my buddy. While I was tattooing him, we got talking about how my life had changed and what I have been up to. I told him about the baptism and how they went. He asked who was baptized, and it turned out that I baptized his ex-wife.

Part of their downfall was over religion. It woke him up inside as we spoke about it, which allowed me to speak the gospel to him. It was just as his wife had said it would be. After that tattoo, I gave it up for good. The outreach started growing. God was doing amazing things in the community. We kept praying, and He kept intervening. My wife caught a post on Facebook one afternoon from a kid who was known to be involved in drugs. His post was dramatic as if he was going to end his life. Something happened that day though that was the beginning of a special season for us. A few comments down on his post, he said that something crazy happened to him. He wanted to know if there was anyone who knew about hearing God speak. I knew his family well, so Shana reached out and asked him to come over to our apartment that night. He came over and told us how a woman he knew approached him while he was at a nearby creek, contemplating about ending his life. She prayed for him, and he heard God telling him to get up and go home. He felt something inside that gave him a hope he never had before. We broke out a couple of Bibles and read some of the gospels. He soaked it up like a sponge. He started going to church with us that Sunday.

A year earlier, a woman came in to the Outreach and asked if I could save her son. She said she didn't like me, but I was her only hope. I told her that I couldn't save anyone, but I would be glad to pray with her because Jesus could. Our prayers were answered when her son ended up in the hospital with a serious issue. While he was there, God spoke to him. He messaged us asking when our meetings were, and sure enough he started coming to them.

Another guy who came around in the beginning also had an encounter with God while in a police car on his way to the hospital after an episode with drugs. Those three young men began to turn things upside down.

We started doing life with them, having them over for dinner, and just to hang out. That summer, God moved mountains. I ended up going to the local prisons to minister to a few people who were looking for help. People were coming out of the woodwork, both to seek help and to help us out. We heard some of the saddest stories during that time but watched God redeem what the enemy had stolen.

Speaking of the enemy, our cycle shop was costing us valuable time and money, and it looked as though we needed to close it down. It had its purpose though; it gave people a place to come talk outside of the outreach. We watched God move there too from helping a suicidal kid to even being part of one of the biggest busts in that town to date. We knew it was time for me to go into full-time ministry, so Shana got a job as a caretaker for a friend's elderly dad, and we shut the shop down.

I was free to minister, study, pray, and work with other pastors. That wasn't easy though. Many pastors in town didn't accept me as a legitimate minister. God was doing so much at the outreach I really didn't care, but God did. Through one episode after another, He brought us into friendships that were centered in Christ. It wasn't easy though. Many hurt feelings needed healed, and many trips to the woodshed and the potter's wheel were on my schedule. Shana eventually got a word from the Lord that it was time to step into full-time ministry. She was burning the candle at both ends, and it was wearing her down. She wrestled over the word to quit for a little while, but one day in the bathroom, God spoke again. She asked why He wasn't providing financially for us. His answer was profound and launched us into one of the busiest seasons we ever had. He told her because she was trusting in her own provision, and she need to trust Him. She did, and He came through as He always does.

Our time in Emporium was amazing with a constant battle between good and evil. We have since relocated to Harrisburg for a couple years and then Northwestern Philly for the last two years. Ministry has been amazing, God has done so much, and the battle still rages.

But for the sake of keeping this book at a reasonable length, I have decided to write another book of God's works of grace from the testimonies we have been blessed to witness during our time in ministry. To bring this book to a close, I would like to summarize my experience with God's grace. I have done an enormous amount of stupid, hurtful, and downright evil things. Some of which I couldn't write down. I have served the devil in many capacities. But when it comes down to it, the love of God and His abundant grace are no match for my fallen nature. After that head-on collision with Him, His grace not only forgave me but is continually transforming me into who I was created to be.

There's absolutely nothing special about me other than maybe my uncanny ability to screw up, which should make it even more obvious that God's grace is for anybody and everybody. To God be the glory through the works of His Son, Jesus Christ, by the power of the Holy Spirit. Amen.

"For God so loved the world, that He gave His only begotten son, that whoever believes in Him shall not perish, but have eternal life" (John 3:16 NASB).

ABOUT THE AUTHOR

Daniel, a former drug dealer and now the cofounder of Painted Soldier Ministry, is a renowned speaker from Pennsylvania, teaching and telling his story of God's grace in many platforms. An evangelist, author, and podcaster, he is dedicated to making a difference in people's lives around the world. Daniel has now put his travels and experiences down in print for others to be motivated to do the same.

Before

After